6/14

THE LIBRARY OF
AMERICAN
LIVES AND TIMES™

BENEDICT ARNOLD

Revolutionary War
Hero and Traitor

Dr. Walter L. Powell

The Rosen Publishing Group's
PowerPlus Books™
New York

To my father, who gave me my love of history,
to my wife and best friend Sue, and to my best
literary critics, my children Nat and Sally!

Published in 2004 by The Rosen Publishing Group, Inc.
29 East 21st Street, New York, NY 10010

First Edition

Editor's Note: All quotations have been reproduced as they appeared in
the letters and diaries from which they were borrowed. No correction was
made to the inconsistent spelling that was common in that time period.

Library of Congress Cataloging-in-Publication Data

Powell, Walter Louis.
  Benedict Arnold : revolutionary war hero and traitor / Walter L. Powell.
    p. cm.—(The library of American lives and times)
  Includes bibliographical references and index.
  Contents: Childhood—New Haven merchant—Off to war—The march
to Quebec—Retreat from Canada and the Battle of Valcour Island—Hero
of Ridgefield and Saratoga—Military governor of Philadelphia—Treason
at West Point—Benedict Arnold, British general—Last years in Canada
and England.
  ISBN 0-8239-6627-5 (library binding)
1. Arnold, Benedict, 1741–1801—Juvenile literature. 2. American loyalists—Biography—Juvenile literature. 3. Generals—United States—
Biography—Juvenile literature. 4. United States. Continental Army—
Biography—Juvenile literature. 5. United States—History—Revolution,
1775–1783—Juvenile literature. [1. Arnold, Benedict, 1741–1801. 2.
American loyalists. 3. Generals. 4. United States—History—Revolution,
1775–1783.] I. Title. II. Series.
  E278.A7P69 2004
  973.3'092—dc21
  [B]

                                        2002011915

Manufactured in the United States of America

CONTENTS

Introduction

Along the banks of the Thames River, a short distance from Westminster Abbey in London, stands a red brick church called St. Mary's. Built in 1777, the church is almost hidden now by larger buildings. Few passersby know that America's most famous traitor, Benedict Arnold, is buried in the crypt under the church.

If Benedict Arnold's last resting place is largely forgotten, Arnold himself is certainly remembered. Few people in American history are hated as much as he is, and his name is still associated with treason against the people of the United States. This wasn't always true. During the early years of the American Revolution, Arnold was admired for his courage and leadership. Many Americans believed that Arnold was largely responsible for the defeat of British general John Burgoyne in October 1777. This victory at the Battle of Saratoga gave Americans the momentum they needed to win the war. Had Arnold died

Opposite: This portrait of Benedict Arnold was contained in a locket worn by Arnold's second wife, Peggy Shippen. The portrait was painted around 1782, after Arnold's defection to the British. Arnold wears the red uniform of a British officer.

of the leg wound he suffered in that battle, he would be remembered as one of America's greatest heroes.

How could a man who risked his life for his country choose to betray it? There is no simple answer, and trying to explain Arnold's motives based on greed or a desire for revenge is not enough. It may help to understand that, at the time, the notion of joining the colonies to create a union of states was still new. Many people remained uneasy about separating from Britain. Perhaps as many as one-third of Americans remained loyal to the British Crown during the war, and large numbers had to flee to Britain or Canada after the British were defeated.

The American Revolution was America's first civil war, and numerous families were torn apart by the conflict. For example, no American was better known or more committed to the Revolution than was Benjamin Franklin, but his son William was the British royal governor of New Jersey. William never spoke to his father again once the war started.

Despite what some biographers would later claim, Benedict Arnold was not born to be a traitor. Nevertheless, the choices he made would have a lasting impact on his life, on the lives of those he loved, and on the lives of his countrymen. The powerful lesson to be learned is that the actions of one person can affect countless people, for good or for ill.

1. Childhood

Benedict Arnold was born in Norwich, Connecticut, on January 14, 1741. He was part of the fifth generation of his family to live in America. His great-great-great-grandfather, William Arnold, had come from England to the Massachusetts Bay colony in the early 1630s, seeking a better life and religious freedom. In 1636, not happy with the religious leaders of Massachusetts Bay, William joined Roger Williams in establishing the colony of Rhode Island. William's son became wealthy in the colony and was elected governor.

William's descendant Benedict Arnold IV, father of the future traitor, spent his youth as a cooper's apprentice in Providence, Rhode Island. The idea of working as a barrel maker for the rest of his life did not appeal to him, so in 1730, Benedict and his brother Oliver headed for Norwich, Connecticut.

Founded in 1659, Norwich was quickly growing into one of the largest seaport towns in Connecticut. The same year that Benedict and Oliver arrived, four sloops owned by Norwich sea captains were trading along the Atlantic

This 1851 daguerreotype of Benedict Arnold's birthplace in Norwich, Connecticut, was taken by E. Z. Webster. The winter that Benedict was born was one of the coldest on record. Freezing temperatures would rarely bother Benedict, whose childhood winters were spent outdoors ice skating.

coast, and with Europe and the West Indies. Captain Absalom King hired the Arnold brothers to work for him. In September 1732, on a return trip from Ireland, Captain King died at sea. The following year, Benedict married the captain's young widow, Hannah, and gained not only the substantial wealth left by Captain King but also the ties to Hannah's influential relatives, the Watermans and the Lathrops.

Hannah and Benedict's first child, Benedict, was born in August 1738, but he died less than a year later. During this time when infant mortality was high, couples often gave the same name to another child, as the Arnolds did for their next son. After young Benedict was born in 1741, the Arnolds had four more children: Hannah, Mary, Absalom King, and Elizabeth.

Historians have few details of Benedict's childhood. In the 1850s, Norwich town historian Frances Manwaring Caulkins concluded that he was "bold, enterprising, ambitious, active as lightning, and with a ready wit always at command."

Young Benedict probably spent much of his time on the waterfront. There he could watch his father, who was known as Captain Arnold, supervising the loading and unloading of his ships' cargoes. Captain Arnold's ships often made two or more round-trips per year to the West Indies. In Norwich, the ships were loaded with beef, pork, butter, cheese, bread, fish, onions, horses, mules, and lumber. They returned from the West Indies with molasses, sugar, rum, coffee, salt, tropical fruits, and cocoa.

In the fall of 1752, when Benedict was eleven, his parents sent him to a boarding school in nearby Canterbury, Connecticut. The school was run by the Reverend James Cogswell, a Yale College graduate and one of Hannah's cousins. Hannah had great respect for Cogswell's teaching ability. She knew that her restless son would get the discipline and education that he needed to be admitted as a student at Yale. Benedict's mother wrote to her son often. Her

A MAP of
the most INHABITED part of
VIRGINIA
containing the whole PROVINCE of
MARYLAND
with Part of
PENSILVANIA, NEW JERSEY AND NORTH CAROLINA
Drawn by
Joshua Fry & Peter Jefferson
in 1751.

This engraving is a detail from a map done by Joshua Fry and Peter Jefferson in 1751. It was later used as a cartouche in the 1777 *North American Atlas*. A cartouche was a small illustration that adorned a map. The scene depicts a busy dock where barrels of tobacco bound for foreign ports are being sealed and loaded onto merchant ships. The men at the center of the engraving are probably merchants or members of the ship's crew, chatting and having a drink after negotiating a price for the tobacco.

letters tell us much about Hannah's religious devotion and her concern for her son's spiritual welfare. On August 13, 1753, she wrote of a serious outbreak of disease in Norwich that had already killed several people. Hannah warned her son, "Pray my dear, whatever you neglect do not neglect your precious soul which once lost can never be regained." On August 30, his mother anxiously wrote that his sisters Mary and Elizabeth were sick, his father was ill, and that "I myself had a touch of the distemper."

Mrs. Arnold's concerns about her family's health were well founded. She and her husband watched helplessly as the two girls became increasingly ill and then died. Perhaps because of this tragedy, Benedict became closely devoted to his surviving sister, Hannah.

In 1754, when Benedict was thirteen, his mother pulled him out of school. She could no longer afford the tuition, as Benedict's father was having financial difficulties. Some biographers believe that the death of his two daughters was too much for Captain Arnold to bear. This man, who had once been a respected member of the Norwich business community and the First Congregational Church, became known as a drunk.

Benedict Senior's alcoholism forced Mrs. Arnold to take charge of the family finances and to find a way to continue Benedict's education. She approached her cousins, Daniel and Joshua Lathrop, who agreed to take on Benedict as an apprentice in their Norwich apothecary shop. In the 1700s, apothecaries prepared drugs and medications, as do pharmacists today. However, apothecaries offered many other goods. The Lathrop brothers were well-known apothecaries and businessmen in Norwich and the surrounding area. They were among the wealthiest citizens of the town. Benedict respected the Lathrops, who found him to be intelligent and an eager and reliable worker. Under their supervision, he gained the eighteenth-century equivalent of a complete business education.

In August 1759, Arnold's mother died. Benedict loved his mother and never entirely recovered from her death. Young Benedict also never forgot the humiliation of seeing his father lose the family fortune and the community's respect. When his father died in 1761, Benedict remained in town just long enough to complete the terms of his apprenticeship. After he turned twenty-one in January 1762, Benedict Arnold left Norwich, never to live there again.

2. New Haven Merchant

In the spring of 1762, Benedict Arnold sailed for London. The Lathrops had made him a business partner and had given him instructions to open another apothecary shop in Connecticut. The Lathrops gave Arnold letters of introduction to important London merchants. When Arnold returned to America with the store goods he had purchased, he came to New Haven, another important seaport and the third-largest town in Connecticut. The community was known for its intellectual and religious diversity. New Haven was home to several churches, Yale College, and Connecticut's first newspaper.

Arnold stayed with his uncle Oliver until he found lodging and a suitable location to establish his shop. He soon rented property on Chapel Street and set out a sign in front of his shop.

If Arnold could not go to Yale, at least he could profit from those who did. It is not surprising that his first shop was located close to the campus. The Latin motto *Sibi Totique*, meaning "for himself and for all," appeared on his sign and gave the impression that the owner was an

This was the original sign that Benedict Arnold hung above the entrance to his apothecary shop on Chapel Street in New Haven, Connecticut. In addition to selling medicine, surgical tools, and books, Arnold attracted female customers by selling jewelry and a variety of cosmetics from London, such as cold cream and rose water.

educated man. Along with medicines, the goods he offered included a wide assortment of books, which were sure to be of interest to students and other educated men in the community.

Arnold was eager to gain the respect of the important men in New Haven. As did many Americans, Arnold associated success with making money, and he sought additional opportunities to turn a profit. By 1764, Arnold had entered into a partnership with Adam Babcock, another New Haven merchant. Together they purchased the ship *Fortune*. A year later the partners bought two more ships and put them to use by trading for goods in the West Indies and Canada. Like his father, Arnold soon came to be called Captain. As Arnold's business interests grew, he asked his sister Hannah if she would move in with him and manage his business in New Haven while he traveled.

This colonial-era ventilated jar was used by apothecaries to hold leeches. Medical practitioners believed that allowing a leech to suck a patient's blood would draw harmful toxins from the body.

Arnold's business ventures continued to expand throughout the 1760s. These were turbulent years in both America and Europe. The French and Indian War in America began in 1754 and ended with the Treaty of Paris in 1763. The defeated French gave Canada to Britain, which then became the greatest power in Europe. The cost of waging the war, however, had nearly doubled the British national debt. George III, king of Great Britain, and his advisers felt that some of this money ought to be recovered by taxing the British colonies in North America. As a result, from 1763 to 1765, the king and Parliament passed several laws to increase British control over colonial trade and to collect more taxes from the colonists. The most controversial of the laws were the Sugar Act of 1764 and the Stamp Act of 1765.

The Sugar Act reduced the tax on molasses but increased it on other goods and raised the fines for ship owners who failed to pay the required tax. The Stamp Act required that all public documents, whether printed or written, be prepared on prestamped paper, for which a tax would be charged. Therefore, newspapers, deeds, business contracts, and wills were taxed.

Colonial merchants were not happy with these new regulations. By law, merchants had always been required to pay a tax on goods imported from any country other

An engraver submitted this 1765 proof sheet of official stamps to the Commissioners of Stamps. Once the stamps were inspected and approved by the commissioner, they were used on newspapers and other printed materials in accordance with the British Stamp Act.

than Britain. In practice, though, many merchants did what they could to evade the law. This was possible because customs officials often smuggled goods themselves or took bribes to accept false information about a ship's contents.

When Arnold's ship the *Fortune* returned from the West Indies in January 1766, Arnold planned to avoid paying the tax on molasses. His plan might have succeeded, but one of his sailors, Peter Boles, threatened to tell customs officials unless he received more pay. Arnold refused his demand, and Boles went to a customs official to seek a reward as an informer. When Arnold found out, he took several of his crew, cornered Boles at a local tavern, and threatened him. A few days later, Arnold forced Boles to sign a confession stating that he had lied about the content of Arnold's cargo and to agree to leave town immediately. When Boles failed to leave, Arnold and his men carried Boles to a public whipping post and whipped him with forty lashes on the back. Boles quickly fled town, never to return.

The public officials of New Haven, who were still loyal to Britain, were horrified by the incident. On January 31, a grand jury indicted Arnold and nine of his men for the crime of disturbing the peace. News of the indictment traveled quickly, and that evening Arnold and a large group of citizens gathered to protest on New Haven Green. After listening to several speeches condemning the Stamp Act, the crowd paraded by torchlight through the streets of New Haven. They carried a full-size model of a gallows with effigies, or likenesses, of the two grand jurors who had indicted Arnold hanging from the gallows. When the parade was over, they tossed the effigies into a large bonfire.

Arnold was found guilty and was fined fifty shillings. He paid the fine but continued to protest. He argued that the unjust British laws and the men who threatened to become informants could cause financial ruin for New Haven businesses. To many, Arnold had become a public hero and a defender of liberties. At the age of twenty-five, Arnold had made his mark in New Haven.

Though Arnold had his share of enemies who disliked his politics and his rapid rise as a merchant, others admired him, including Colonel Nathan Whiting, a distinguished veteran of the French and Indian War. Whiting introduced him to the men of his social circle, including Samuel Mansfield, the high sheriff of New Haven County. Mansfield had a twenty-one-year-old daughter named Margaret who soon caught Arnold's eye. They began courting in the fall of 1766, and the following February they were married. Arnold had improved his status by marrying into a prominent family. By all accounts, Margaret Mansfield, nicknamed Peggy, was his first love. During the next six years, the couple had three children: Benedict VI, Richard, and Henry.

Arnold developed plans to build a suitable house to provide ample room for his growing family and to reflect his increasing wealth and importance. In 1770, construction began on a 3-acre (1-ha) property on Water Street. The house was a two-story structure, built in the fashionable Georgian style, with large brick chimneys, a porch with pillars on both sides of the front door, and large windows.

In the years leading up to the American Revolution, Arnold continued to support protests against British policies. Though often abroad on business, he stayed as well informed as he could. When he learned that British troops in Boston had killed five civilians during the so-called Boston Massacre of March 5, 1770, he wrote to his

This photo of Benedict Arnold's home in New Haven, Connecticut, was taken in the 1890s. Arnold hoped that the two pillars outside the front entrance would give visitors the impression that this was the residence of an important gentleman. Behind the house were gardens, a stable, and a coach house.

friend Benjamin Douglas, "Good God! Are the Americans all asleep and calmly giving up their glorious liberties, or are they all turned philosophers, that they don't take immediate vengeance on such miscreants!"

In 1773, the British passed the Tea Act, which created a tea monopoly for the British East India Tea Company. The citizens of Boston responded by staging the famous Boston Tea Party. Costumed as Indians, Americans dumped 342 chests of East India Tea into Boston Harbor. King George and Parliament responded by closing the port of Boston, and by ordering additional British troops to America. Concerned that war with Britain was likely, sixty-five New Haven citizens organized into a militia company in December 1774. They petitioned the general assembly of Connecticut and asked to be officially recognized as the Governor's Second Company of Guards. This company of men was also known as the Foot Guards. The general assembly agreed, and on March 15, 1775, the company elected officers, choosing Benedict Arnold as their captain. The outbreak of the American Revolution was just a month away, and with it, Arnold's opportunity to prove himself as a soldier.

3. Off to War

The conflict with Britain became a full-scale war on the morning of April 19, 1775. British regulars, sent from Boston to seize colonial military supplies hidden in Concord, clashed with Captain John Parker's militia company on the town green in Lexington, Massachusetts. The British scattered Parker's men and marched on to Concord. They were met by another group of militia, larger than the first, who forced the British into a long and bloody retreat back to Boston.

News of the Battle of Lexington and Concord reached New Haven on April 21. After a heated discussion, the townsmen voted by a narrow majority not to send military aid to the Massachusetts rebels. Benedict Arnold ignored these orders. Knowing that his Governor's Second Company of Guards supported him, he assembled the men, who agreed to leave for Massachusetts the next day.

On Saturday morning, April 22, Arnold headed for New Haven Green, where his company had gathered on his order. After inspecting the men, Arnold sent a request

The Engagement at the North Bridge was created by Amos Doolittle in 1775. The painting depicts the fateful meeting of British troops and the Continental militia on the North Bridge in Concord, Massachusetts. About two hundred British regulars fought against approximately four hundred American militia. The British were forced to retreat.

to the selectmen, the town's governing officials, for a supply of gunpowder from the town powder house. At first the selectmen refused, but when Captain Arnold threatened to break down the door and take what he needed, they gave him the keys. The company marched to the headquarters of the Massachusetts provincial army at Cambridge.

Once he and his men arrived, Arnold wasted little time sitting around. He did not want his men to join a siege of the British forces in Boston. After finding housing for his men, he presented a plan to the Massachusetts Committee of Safety to attack Fort Ticonderoga. The fort was located at the lower end of Lake Champlain in upstate New York and controlled the water passages between Lake George and Lake Champlain. The French had built the fort in 1755 and called it Fort Carillon.

When the French evacuated and blew up Fort Carillon in 1759, the British rebuilt it and renamed it Fort Ticonderoga. After the war, the British maintained a small garrison in the fort to guard the gunpowder and cannons stored there. Arnold argued that it would be easy to overwhelm the small garrison in a surprise attack and seize the much-needed supplies.

The Committee of Safety saw the merits of Arnold's plan and gave him a commission as a colonel, with instructions to recruit an additional force of four hundred Massachusetts soldiers to attack the fort. What Arnold did not know, however, was that Ethan Allen, the commander of the Green Mountain Boys of Vermont, was already planning an attack with the financial support of several prominent Connecticut men.

When Arnold reached Stockbridge, Massachusetts, to begin his recruiting, he learned of Allen's plan and hurried ahead to Castleton, Vermont, to stop him. The government of Massachusetts had authorized Arnold's commission, but Allen had only informal instructions from some Connecticut patriots. Both Arnold and Allen were eager for glory and respect.

f

f

f

f

f

f

f

f

f

f

f

f

f

Juts
Carrillon
Will

On May 9, 1775, Ethan Allen's force of some two hundred men gathered at Hands Cove, about 2 miles (3 km) north of Fort Ticonderoga on Lake Champlain, and waited for boats to take them across. Arnold caught up with Allen there and insisted that he take command.

Arnold had met his match, however. Ethan Allen was a thirty-seven-year-old veteran of the French and Indian War and a native of Connecticut. He had made his military reputation in the ongoing colonial border dispute between New York and New Hampshire over lands that eventually became the state of Vermont. In 1770, Allen was elected colonel commandant of a group of rough frontiersmen who called themselves the Green Mountain Boys. Allen was not about to take orders from anyone. When Arnold remained insistent, Allen's men made it clear that they would not listen to Arnold. Finally, Allen suggested that Arnold could serve beside him in a joint command. Arnold unwillingly agreed.

The bigger problem of how to cross Lake Champlain remained. Allen had sent out a raiding party the day before to capture a small schooner. When the raiding party returned, all they brought was a single 33-foot (10-m) bateau. With wind and rain kicking up, crossing the lake would not be easy. If Allen was to surprise the British garrison at Fort Ticonderoga before daylight, the

Opposite: This 1777 map of Fort Carillon, which later became Fort Ticonderoga, was drawn by Michel du Chesnoy. This close-up of the map highlights the strategic placement of the fort along the banks of Lake Champlain.

Bateaux, such as these shown above, were small flat-bottomed boats. Arnold and Allen were able to secure only one boat for their attack on Fort Ticonderoga. This drawing by Sydney Adamson, which shows Arnold and his men in bateaux during a later expedition to invade British-held Canada, was later made into an engraving by Harry Davidson in 1903.

men would have to leave soon. Arnold, who had more experience handling boats, suggested that there was only time to ferry across two groups of about forty men before dawn. The rest could follow later. Allen agreed, and the two led the first bateau across.

At about 4:00 A.M., Arnold and Allen gathered a group of eighty-three men a short distance from Fort Ticonderoga's boat landing, then moved in silence up a slope toward the main fort. Arnold, sword in hand, rushed toward the single British sentry, or guard, who was asleep at his post. Startled, the sentry pulled the trigger of his musket, but the gun misfired. The sentry ran back for the main gate. Both Allen and Arnold would later claim that they sped toward the sentry at the same time. Other soldiers who had witnessed the event, however, concluded that it was Arnold who had reached the man first.

Accounts of what happened next vary considerably. Allen wrote the best-known version, claiming that he overpowered a second sentry, then demanded that the soldier lead him to the commandant's quarters. Moving to the staircase of the west barracks, Allen pushed the sentry aside, rushed up the stairs, and, standing at the door

This hand-colored engraving by Alonzo Chappel dramatizes Ethan Allen's account of the capture of Fort Ticonderoga. Although Benedict Arnold and Ethan Allen captured the fort together, the artist has not included Arnold in his depiction of the event.

of Captain William Delaplace's quarters, asked him to "come forth instantly or I would sacrifice the whole garrison." Allen wrote that Captain Delaplace came to the door, half asleep, and asked Allen "by what authority I demanded it." Allen replied, "In the name of the great Jehovah, and the Continental Congress!"

The British account of the attack, written by Lieutenant Jocelyn Feltham, second in command, claimed that when Allen's men arrived they were completely disorganized. Feltham deliberately stood by the second floor doorway of his quarters to catch Allen's and Arnold's attention. Trying to stall them, Feltham demanded to know by what authority they entered "his majesties fort." According to Feltham's account, Arnold and Allen announced that they would take immediate control of the fort and everything in it.

Allen, believing that Feltham was in command, held a sword over his head and threatened that if the fort did not surrender "neither man woman or child should be left alive in the fort." Feltham also noted that by contrast, Benedict Arnold demanded surrender in a "genteel manner, but without success."

Captain Delaplace finally came out and agreed to surrender after Arnold and Allen assured him that his soldiers and their families would be treated as prisoners of war. Once Fort Ticonderoga had been captured, Arnold's dispute with Allen began again. Arnold was unhappy with the Green Mountain Boys, who celebrated their victory by looting the possessions of the British soldiers and their families and getting drunk. When Arnold tried to stop them, some of Allen's men threatened to shoot him. Thoroughly frustrated, Arnold confined himself to the officer's quarters and wrote a report of the incident to Joseph Warren of the Massachusetts Committee of Safety. He advised Warren that "Colonel Allen is a proper man to head his own wild people, but entirely unacquainted with military service. As I am the only person who has been legally authorized to take possession of this place, I am determined to insist upon my right."

Arnold's attitude had angered not only Allen but also two other men on the expedition, James Easton and John Brown. Easton, a tavern keeper from Pittsfield, Massachusetts, and Allen's friend, thought he, Easton, should have been commissioned to head the Massachusetts volunteers who had attacked the fort. John Brown, a lawyer, had a personal dislike for Arnold's family. He had once worked for Arnold's cousin Oliver in Rhode Island and had been fired. When Ethan Allen wrote his report of the attack for the Massachusetts Provincial Congress, he claimed that Easton led the Massachusetts men "with great zeal and fortitude" and that John Brown was "personally in the attack" when he was actually across Lake Champlain at the time. Allen sent Easton to Cambridge to deliver his report, making sure that Arnold's name was not mentioned. All three men hoped to discredit Arnold's role in the campaign.

Arnold's capture and destruction of the British naval ships at St. Johns in May 1775 delayed the enemy's advance into the Lake Champlain region. As both Fort Ticonderoga and Crown Point were surrounded by water, Arnold believed the forts would remain secure until the British could build a new fleet. This painting of St. Johns was created by Thomas Anburey in 1789.

Though this effort angered Arnold, he tried not to allow his feelings to distract him from his sense of duty. He was concerned that the fort would not be safe from a British counterattack unless the Americans had naval control of Lake Champlain. An opportunity to seize control of the lake developed when Captain Eleazar Oswald, a member of Arnold's Foot Guard, arrived at Fort Ticonderoga with the schooner *Katherine* on May 14. Arnold proposed to use the *Katherine* to sail down Lake Champlain and attack the town of St. Johns, Canada, near the mouth of the Richelieu River, where a small

British garrison protected the sloop *George*, the only British warship on Lake Champlain.

At a council of war held on the afternoon of May 14, Allen and his officers agreed to Arnold's proposal. Renaming the schooner *Liberty*, Arnold sailed down Lake Champlain and arrived at St. Johns early on the morning of May 18. He caught the small British garrison by surprise and within a few hours captured thirteen soldiers, their arms and powder, nine bateaux, and the sloop *George*, which was armed with two cannons. Concerned that British reinforcements might be close by, Arnold destroyed five bateaux, gathered his prisoners, and sailed back to Lake Champlain that afternoon.

In late May 1775, both Allen and Arnold discussed a plan to invade Canada. If the two men had any thoughts about the Second Continental Congress supporting such a plan, they were quickly discouraged. On May 28, news arrived that Congress did not want to maintain Fort Ticonderoga or Crown Point. Congress asked that the colonial forces pull back to Lake George.

Determined not to give up on his plans to invade Canada, Arnold wrote a letter to the Continental Congress on June 13, suggesting that an army of two thousand men under his command could take Montreal and Quebec. Arnold soon had other problems to occupy him, however. In response to Easton's vocal criticism of Arnold in Cambridge, the Massachusetts Provincial

Congress had appointed a committee to investigate Arnold's conduct.

This news came as a shock to Arnold, who felt that he had gone beyond the call of duty. On June 23, Arnold resigned his commission in disgust. Before going home, he agreed to travel to Albany. There, at General Philip Schuyler's request, he submitted a report to the Continental Congress on the condition of troops and defenses at Ticonderoga and Crown Point.

Biographer Willard Wallace later wrote, "Arnold's heart was no longer in this work. He felt his honor impugned by what had happened, and his pride was sorely hurt." The final blow, however, was the news that his wife, Peggy, had died of unknown causes on June 19. Arnold quickly departed for New Haven. It seemed as if his career as a soldier was finished.

4. The March to Quebec

When Arnold returned to New Haven, he was overwhelmed by the burdens facing him. Peggy's death left him with three motherless children, and the outbreak of war had taken a toll on his New Haven business and shipping interests. Although Arnold had spent a great deal of his own money on food and supplies for his soldiers, the Massachusetts Provincial Congress questioned his expenses. Arnold was frustrated, but still eager to prove that he deserved another command and credit for the successes at Fort Ticonderoga and St. Johns. Always restless, Arnold remained in New Haven for just two weeks. Hannah promised to take care of his children and to manage his business affairs. He left for Watertown, Massachusetts, to meet with the Provincial Congress and to defend the expenses he had generated during his time on Lake Champlain.

Arnold made his presentation to the Massachusetts Congress on August 1, 1775, but they referred the matter to a special committee. While Arnold waited for a reply, he arranged a meeting with General George Washington, the new commander of the Continental army, at his head-quarters in Cambridge.

Washington, familiar with Arnold's efforts on Lake Champlain, took an immediate liking to this young man. When Arnold urged the general to invade Canada, Washington listened with great interest. Washington had become acquainted with the proposed invasion route up the Kennebec, Dead, and Chaudière Rivers to Quebec during the French and Indian War.

Unknown to Arnold, General Philip Schuyler, reacting to Arnold's earlier report to him in Albany, had made plans to attack Canada. Washington wrote to Schuyler asking his opinion of Arnold and of the plan to launch an attack on Quebec. Schuyler replied with a strong approval of both.

For ten days, Washington and Arnold worked fever-ishly to organize the expedition. On September 3, 1775, Washington ordered Reuben Colburn, a shipbuilder in Gardinerstown, Maine, to construct two hundred bateaux and to gather supplies for one thousand men. Washington offered Arnold a commission as colonel in the Continental army and issued a general order on September 5 for vol-unteers to serve on the expedition.

On September 6, hundreds of inexperienced volun-teers arrived at Washington's camp at Cambridge. General Horatio Gates selected about 786 of these men and divided them into two battalions of five companies each. Lieutenant Colonel Roger Enos would command

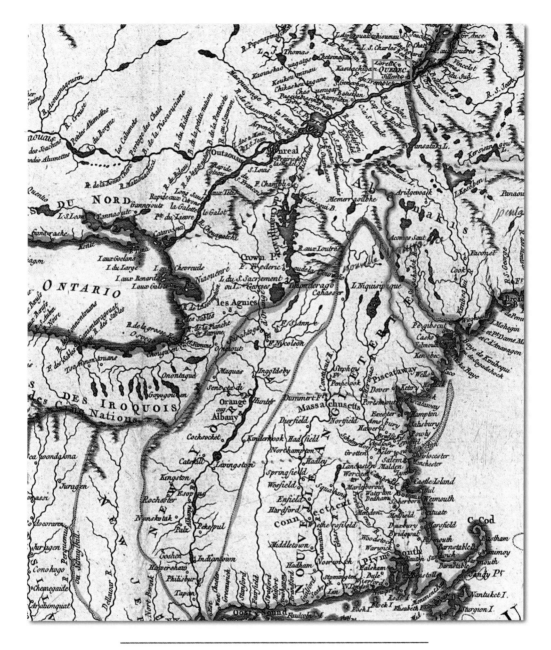

Gilles Robert de Vaugondy's map, which shows portions of Canada and the United States, was published in France in 1778. The American invasion route up the Kennebec, Dead, and Chaudière Rivers to Quebec has been highlighted by colored lines. The Kennebec is colored blue, the Dead is red, and the Chaudière is purple. Quebec, at the top of the map, is highlighted by a green box.

the first battalion, and Lieutenant Colonel Christopher Greene would lead the second. Also joining Arnold were three hundred experienced frontier riflemen from Virginia and Pennsylvania, commanded by Captains Daniel Morgan, William Hendricks, and Matthew Smith. With a few additional volunteers, Arnold's force numbered about 1,050 men.

The men left Cambridge by ship on or before September 13 and arrived at Gardinerstown, Maine, on September 22. Here Arnold realized that the expedition would be more difficult than he had imagined. A drought had made the Kennebec River too shallow in many places for the heavy bateaux to float. Moreover, Arnold was shocked to find that the two hundred new bateaux were poorly built. Biographer Willard Sterne Randall wrote, "the result was a meadow full of ill-suited, badly made, undersized, overweight boats to carry Arnold's Army through 400 miles [644 km] of rough water and portages to Quebec."

Arnold had no choice but to move ahead. He set out from Fort Western in late September. Ahead of him were scouts, accompanied by local guides. On the first leg of the trip, from Fort Western to Skowhegan, Maine, numerous rapids and waterfalls on the Kennebec River forced the men to portage, or carry, the bateaux until they reached calmer water. The task was backbreaking, as each bateau alone weighed 400 pounds (181 kg). There were settlements along the Kennebec where

Benedict Arnold's men portage their bateaux at Skowhegan Falls in this 1903 C. W. Chadwick engraving created from a drawing done by Sydney Adamson around 1780. As the men struggled to lift their heavy boats, Arnold cheered them on with the rallying cry, "To Quebec and victory."

Arnold asked for assistance. Once he departed from Skowhegan, however, his journey was through nearly 300 miles (483 km) of largely unmapped forests, swamps, rivers, and lakes.

On the morning of October 2, Arnold learned that many of the bateaux had leaked and water had ruined much of the food. In the eighteenth century, meats such as beef and pork were sealed in wooden barrels of salt water to prevent spoilage. Many barrels had become waterlogged and had burst open, spoiling the meat and ruining the flour. Arnold ordered his men to repair the bateaux and to salvage as much food as possible. This delayed the expedition another week. Meanwhile, the weather turned bitter cold at night and the food supplies dwindled.

The expedition continued on October 9 toward Carratunk Falls, Maine, then on to an area called the Great Carrying Place. From there, 8 miles (13 km) of portage and 4 miles (6.4 km) of rowing across ponds took them, after seven days travel, to the Dead River.

Many of the men had become sick. At the urging of Dr. Isaac Senter, Arnold left a small group of soldiers behind to build a log hospital. Arnold's men pushed ahead, and the weather got colder. After a hurricane on October 21, Arnold wrote in his diary, "the rapidity of the current renders it almost impossible for the Battoes to ascend the River, or the men to find their way by land . . . [and] our Provisions are almost exhausted. . . ."

Arnold could either turn back, or find a way to stretch his limited food supply. He ordered his rear column under Colonel Enos to accompany the weaker men back to the Maine settlements. The men who remained would move forward with enough food for fifteen days. Enos sent forward some of the supplies, but disobeyed orders by marching back to the settlements with most of his battalion, one-third of the entire command. Arnold's men felt betrayed when they learned the news. The remaining seven hundred men crossed icy swamps to Lake Megantic. By October 31, with no food left, they reached the Chaudière River. Desperate, some of the men killed and ate a pet dog, while others ate their shaving soap, candles, or the leather from their shoes.

Realizing that the situation was critical, Arnold pushed ahead with a small advance party to find supplies. Fortunately, they soon reached the French Canadian village of Sartigan, now called St. Georges, where he was warmly received. He sent 500 pounds (227 kg) of flour back to the main column. Once all of Arnold's men had reached the settlements along the Chaudière River, the march quickened and by November 9, they were gathered at Point Lévis, on the St. Lawrence River opposite Quebec. Four days later, Arnold's men slipped

---

Next spread: This painting of Quebec City was created by George Heriot. In the foreground are a few homes that were burned during the American attack in 1775. The geographic layout of Upper Town, built on a rise, and Lower Town, situated below the rise, is clearly visible.

past British warships in a night crossing. By morning most of his command was assembled on the large open fields facing the stone walls of Quebec City.

Arnold had hoped to attack the city immediately. During a unit inspection, however, he discovered that most of his men had fewer than five rounds of ammunition. He ordered a retreat to Point aux Trembles, 20 miles (32 km) from Quebec. There on December 1, he was joined by General Richard Montgomery's column, which had been sent by General Philip Schuyler to capture Montreal before joining forces with Arnold. When General Montgomery arrived, Arnold turned his command over to his superior. This time, however, there would be no squabbling. Arnold liked Montgomery, who treated him with courtesy and respect.

Their combined forces numbered about 1,100 men. The situation, however, was getting increasingly difficult.

Winter was approaching, supplies were limited, and the enlistments of many of the men would run out at the end of the year. Montgomery also knew that the British garrison at Quebec had recently been strengthened. If he waited until the spring to attack, British reinforcements would probably force him to retreat.

Looking over the defenses of Quebec City, Montgomery and Arnold realized that the thick stone walls and artillery positions of the part of the city called Upper Town would make an attack there nearly hopeless. They agreed that the best chance lay in attacking the weaker defenses along the river at the part of the city called Lower Town, preferably at night, and during a snowstorm. Before dawn on December 31, as a heavy snowfall began, the Americans divided into two columns. General Montgomery's force of about three hundred men and Colonel Arnold's force of about six hundred men would approach the city from different directions. The two columns planned to link up in Lower Town, then storm up the main thoroughfare to Upper Town.

Montgomery's men were the first to set out. At about 4:00 A.M. they came within 50 yards (46 m) of the first barricade along the river. The general rushed ahead with several of his officers, but the British defenders were ready. They opened fire with muskets and cannons. Montgomery, two of his officers, and several men were killed instantly. The acting commander, Colonel Donald Campbell, ordered a retreat.

The Death of General Montgomery in the Attack on Quebec, December 31, 1775 was painted by John Trumbull in 1786. While traveling from Montreal to his new command in Quebec, Montgomery wrote to Philip Schuyler about his longing to be back at home with his wife, Janet, in the Hudson River valley.

This mezzotint of Arnold, who is shown in front of Quebec, was created in 1776. Many of the American troops in Quebec wore the warmer British uniforms that they took after the victory in Montreal. To identify themselves as Americans, the soldiers attached a sprig of hemlock and a piece of paper with the words "LIBERTY OR DEATH" written on it to their hats.

Meanwhile, Arnold's column slipped by the Palace Gate unchallenged and continued toward a narrow street in Lower Town called Sault-au-Matelot, where they ran into a barricade. As Arnold rushed forward, the defenders opened fire and wounded him in the left leg. Realizing he could not go on, Arnold urged his men to follow Captain Morgan's riflemen. Morgan broke through the first barricade then paused until reinforcements arrived. He lost the advantage of surprise, and British soldiers trapped him from the rear. After several hours of desperate street fighting, Morgan and more than four hundred of his men surrendered. At least fifty-one were killed, and another thirty-six were wounded. The attack on Quebec had failed.

5. The Battle of Valcour Island

Few days in the American Revolution were as bleak as New Year's Day 1776. Benedict Arnold lay wounded, and his brave commander, Richard Montgomery, was dead. Had British governor Guy Carleton chosen to attack on this day, the American forces might have been routed. Arnold guessed, however, that the British commander would not leave the warmth and safety of Quebec's city walls to attack him. Luckily, he was correct. In a letter to his sister Hannah on January 6, 1776, he poured out his feelings:

Sir Guy Carleton, engraved here in 1783, expelled any male citizen of Quebec who refused to join the British militia.

> *I have no thoughts of leaving this proud town until I first enter it in triumph. My wound has been exceeding painful, but is now easy, and the surgeons assure me will be well in eight weeks. I know you will be anxious for me. That Providence which has carried me through*

so many dangers is still my protection. I am in the way of my duty and know no fear.

Arnold reorganized his remaining soldiers and their defenses in front of the city. He sent letters to the Continental Congress and to General David Wooster, the ranking American officer in Canada, requesting reinforcements. Arnold hoped another attack on Quebec might still be made before spring.

When reinforcements arrived, giving Arnold almost 1,800 men, the severe winter weather made any major military operation impossible. Temperatures remained below freezing, and many of Arnold's men suffered from frostbite or became sick with pneumonia or influenza.

In February, Arnold learned that the Continental Congress had appointed him a brigadier general in gratitude for his services on the march to Quebec. His pleasure was tempered by the difficulties he faced trying to keep his army together in front of Quebec. The situation didn't improve when General David Wooster arrived from Montreal on April 1. Wooster had known Arnold in New Haven, did not like him, and refused to consult him on military affairs. When Arnold reinjured his leg in a fall from his horse the next day, he requested a temporary leave to Montreal to assume command of American forces there. Wooster was happy to be rid of him.

When Arnold left Quebec on April 12, no one could predict that this event marked the end of American hopes to secure Canada. General Wooster failed to inspire the men and was replaced by General John Thomas on May 1. After inspecting his soldiers, Thomas ordered a withdrawal on May 6. Unfortunately, British reinforcements arrived at the same time and promptly attacked his men. The patriot soldiers fled in panic, leaving behind most of their supplies. Congress relieved Thomas of his duties.

Despite Arnold's obvious abilities, Congress made the political choice to appoint Major General John Sullivan as the new commander of American forces in Canada. Sullivan was a New Hampshire lawyer and politician with an unimpressive military record. Almost at once, Sullivan's forces suffered a major defeat in the Battle of Three Rivers, and by June 13, Arnold was urging Sullivan to make a careful retreat. Five days later, the last American soldiers were evacuated. Arnold galloped to the waterfront at St. Johns, and as the British forces approached, he shot his horse to prevent it from being captured. He then jumped into a nearby boat to make his escape, the last American officer to leave Canada.

The American retreat from Canada marked the beginning of a British plan to divide the colonies in two. One army, under Governor Guy Carleton, would move south through the Champlain valley, while another, under General William Howe, would capture New York City, then move north up the Hudson River valley. Governor Carleton recognized that he could not carry out his part of the plan without seizing naval control of Lake

pte Aquinonton

the French went ...

Isle de St Michel

L A K E

R au Canot

ISLE DE
VALCOUR
almost
one Rock

American Fleet consisting of 15 Vessels

American Line during the attack

the Road in which the British Fleet

Schooner Gates

Twenty Gun Boats

OF T...

Course of the British Fleet from St John

Petite Isle

Inflexible

the Position which the British Fleet

Anchored in during the night

Schooner
Maria

Radeau Thunderer

R. au
Castor

Gondole Royal Convert

Pointe au Sable
48 Miles from Crown Point

G...

t Arnold BY **THE KING'S FLEET** Commanded by *SIR GUY CARLETON*
eleventh of October 1776, *From a Sketch taken by an Officer on the Spot.*
Engrav'd by Wm Faden Charing Cro. &c.

CHAMPLAIN

ART

DE I

REFERENCES.

Nº 1. Inflexible Ship. 2. Carleton Schooner. 3. Maria Schooner. 4. Congress Galley, run a Shore, with other Vessels a blowing up. 5. Washington Galley striking. 6. Gun Boat coming up.

Riviere à la Moelle

Scale of Three Miles

Champlain. The Americans currently held the lake with three armed ships. Arnold guessed correctly, based on his knowledge of Carleton's personality, that the British commander would never risk taking his army toward Fort Ticonderoga without first building a fleet to escort the troop transports. Over the next two months, the British and the Americans furiously built ships in an effort to control Lake Champlain.

The British had an immediate advantage. Carleton had stores of lumber, rope, and canvas for sails, as well as officers of the Royal Navy to supervise construction. By late August, Carleton had completed twenty-nine vessels. Arnold, on the other hand, had few trained seamen and almost no supplies. On July 3, at the urging of Generals Horatio Gates and Philip Schuyler, Congress agreed to provide funds. Arnold was able to purchase naval supplies and recruit skilled shipwrights and carpenters from the coastal towns of New England. As these men gathered at the shipyard at Skenesborough, New York, Arnold's experience with ships proved of great value. In just eight weeks, twelve vessels were completed.

The two fleets made a sharp contrast. Of Arnold's fleet of fifteen ships, eight were little more than large,

---

Previous spread: This map, engraved by William Faden, illustrates the placement of the American and British fleets during the Battle of Valcour Island. Faden based his map upon an eyewitness sketch created by an officer present at the battle. *Inset*: *Arnold's Engagement on Lake Champlain*, created in 1776, depicts the warships during the battle.

flat-bottomed rowboats called gondolas, with forty-four men crowded aboard. Historian Willard Wallace observed that the ships were "sluggish, overgunned, and manned largely by men who had never been aboard ship." The British ships, on the other hand, were "larger, built of seasoned timber, better gunned, and manned by officers and men of the Royal Navy."

When Arnold learned that Carleton's ships were preparing to leave St. Johns, he sailed his fleet to a defensive position in a sheltered cove between Valcour Island and the New York shoreline. Arnold did not want to risk a battle on the open lake, where the larger British fleet could easily surround him. Valcour Island could also serve to hide his ships as the British sailed south to look for him.

On the morning of October 11, 1776, Carleton's British fleet, commanded by Captain Thomas Pringle, sailed south accompanied by dozens of bateaux and canoes carrying more than 4,000 soldiers and 650 Indians. As Arnold had hoped, they sailed right past Valcour Island, and then discovered the American fleet behind them. The British fleet turned about, facing the wind, which gave the advantage to the Americans. Carleton later wrote, ". . . the wind which had been favorable to bring us there . . . prevented our being able to bring our whole force to engage them, as we had a narrow passage to work up, Ship by Ship, exposed to the fire of their whole line."

In June 1997, a team of researchers working with the Lake Champlain Maritime Museum discovered the remains of a gunboat in Lake Champlain. Nautical archaeologists have since verified the vessel as the Spitfire, a gondola from the Continental fleet, which sank during the American retreat from the Battle of Valcour Island.

The Spitfire landed upright upon the floor of the lake and has been well preserved by the deep, dark, cold waters of Lake Champlain. The vessel was first detected using sonar, a method of locating objects by reflecting sound waves off them. Researchers have continued to document the wreck with a special underwater camera that has taken extensive digital and video footage.

The Spitfire was not the first Revolutionary War ship to be retrieved from the depths of Lake Champlain. In 1935, Colonel Lorenzo F. Hagglund, a professional diver and engineer, discovered the sunken gunboat Philadelphia, another vessel from Arnold's fleet, and brought it to the surface. The Philadelphia was donated in 1961 to the Smithsonian Institution in Washington, D.C., where it was installed in a permanent exhibit.

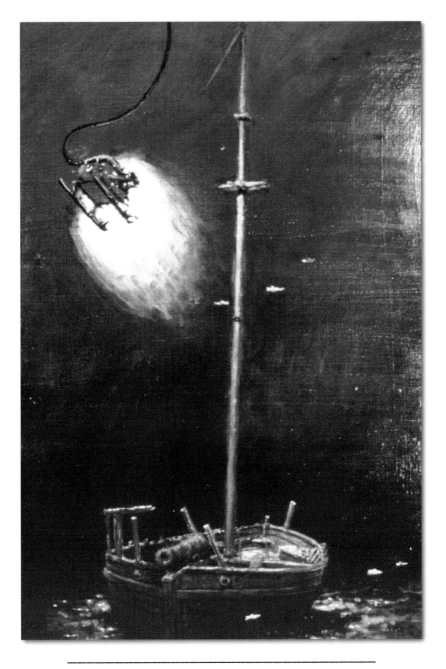

The 1998 painting *The Lost Gunboat* was done by Vermont
marine artist Ernest Haas. The image depicts the special
underwater vehicle that was used to take pictures of the *Spitfire*.

The battle raged for seven hours. Early in the action, a cannon shot hit Captain Pringle's flagship *Maria* and badly wounded Carleton's brother. Another ship, the schooner *Carleton*, lost so many officers and men that a nineteen-year-old midshipman took command.

Arnold's fleet also suffered losses. His largest schooner, the *Royal Savage*, was damaged early in the action and ran aground. The British seized control of her and were able to fire her guns against Arnold's ships. Several of Arnold's gondolas were badly damaged, and one, the *Philadelphia*, sank one hour after the battle was finished.

Captain Pringle pulled his ships out of range at nightfall, and both sides inspected the damage. Arnold had already lost two ships, others were in poor shape, and the Americans had suffered heavy casualties. Fortunately, fog set in that evening, and Arnold was able to slip away to the south and head back toward Fort Ticonderoga. On October 13, however, favorable winds allowed Pringle's fleet to catch up, and in another five-hour battle, the British captured the galley *Washington* and forced Arnold to run ashore at Ferris' Bay, Vermont, with his flagship *Congress* and four other gondolas. Arnold refused to surrender. He defiantly set the ships on fire with their flags still flying and helped to carry the wounded men ashore. Arnold and his men continued overland, linking up with the four remaining ships of his fleet at Fort Ticonderoga on October 14.

Arnold's fleet had been almost completely destroyed, but not in vain. Governor Carleton retreated to St. Johns for the winter. Arnold had bought valuable time for the Continental army, and in the words of naval historian Alfred Thayer Mahan, "never had any force, big or small, lived to better purpose or died more gloriously, for it had saved the lake for that year."

6. Hero of Ridgefield and Saratoga

Benedict Arnold's courage and heroism earned him great praise, even from his enemies. One British publication complimented Arnold's "desperate resistance" and added that he had "raised his character still higher than it was before with his countrymen." Arnold had several jealous critics, however, who claimed that he had sacrificed the American fleet to gain personal glory. Arnold, though sensitive to any charge hinting that he acted dishonorably, put aside his personal concerns because General George Washington required his help.

In December 1776, Washington was camped along the Delaware River north of Philadelphia and had just a fraction of the men he had commanded that summer. His forces had been defeated in New York City, had been driven across the Hudson River to New Jersey, and had been forced across the Delaware River into Pennsylvania. Washington faced the possibility that his army would simply dissolve, as death, disease, and desertion took a steady toll. British general Sir William Howe felt confident that his men would be safe wintering in

New Jersey and could finish off the Continental army in the spring.

As the threat to Fort Ticonderoga was over for the winter, both General Schuyler and General Gates responded to Washington's call for troops. Several Continental regiments began the march south. Moving ahead of those men, Arnold reached Washington's headquarters on December 21, 1776. Washington ordered Arnold to Rhode Island to organize the colonial defenses, as British troops had recently captured Newport.

On his way to Providence, Rhode Island, Arnold had a chance to visit his family in Connecticut. This was the first time he had been home since July 1775. After a short stay, Arnold rode on to Providence, where he recruited and trained soldiers. In Providence, Arnold received a letter from Washington telling him that Congress had promoted five brigadier generals to the rank of major general, but had overlooked Arnold despite Washington's recommendation. Arnold was furious and suspected that his critics had worked behind the scenes to prevent his promotion. Though Washington urged him to be patient, Arnold wrote to Congress and demanded a hearing to make his case. Arnold left for Philadelphia in mid-April, but stopped first in New Haven to spend more time with his family.

On April 26, while still in New Haven, Arnold learned that a large group of British regulars and loyalists commanded by former New York governor

William Tryon had a history of suppressing rebellion in America.
In this nineteenth-century engraving, William Tryon, then the
British governor of North Carolina, is arresting Regulators.
The Regulators were citizens from North Carolina who protested
high taxes and government corruption in a May 1771 rebellion.

William Tryon had landed at Norwalk, Connecticut.
They were heading for Danbury to destroy military
supplies. Arnold joined his old foe General David
Wooster in a hasty effort to recruit militia for the
defense of the state. Rushing north to Redding,
Connecticut, Arnold and Wooster joined a force of
about five hundred men commanded by General Gold
S. Silliman. The officers agreed that although they
could not save Danbury, they would try to prevent the
British from returning to Norwalk and the safety of
their ships.

On the morning of April 27, as Tryon's column left Danbury, General Wooster's militia struck the British rear guard. Wooster was mortally wounded, but his attack gained time for Arnold and Silliman to set up a barricade in Ridgefield. The British struck at about noon. Though outnumbered nearly five to one, Arnold's five hundred untrained militia held their ground, their morale boosted by his leadership. Only after Governor Tryon ordered flanking parties were the patriots overwhelmed and forced to flee. Arnold rode back and forth rallying his troops until his horse was shot, throwing him to the ground and pinning him by one leg. According to one account, a British soldier rushed toward him with a bayonet yelling "Surrender! You are my prisoner." Arnold replied "Not yet," pulled a pistol from his saddle and killed his attacker. He then pulled himself loose from his horse and made his escape.

To stop Tryon's column, Arnold gathered the militia and two artillery detachments at Compo Hill, just 2 miles (3 km) from Norwalk. A relief column of British marines arrived, but not before Arnold's men had inflicted four times as many casualties on the British forces. When news of Arnold's heroism reached Philadelphia on May 2, the Continental Congress finally promoted him to major general.

Meanwhile, a threat of invasion had developed from the British army in Canada. Under the command of John "Gentleman Johnny" Burgoyne, the British

This portrait of General John Burgoyne was painted by Sir Joshua Reynolds around 1766. Burgoyne had been given the nickname Gentleman Johnny by the British soldiers who served under him. His men admired the compassion he granted them. Burgoyne was not a harsh disciplinarian, and he tried to avoid beating his men. The general was also a member of Parliament, a playwright, and an amateur actor.

prepared to move south toward Albany. Burgoyne intended to join the British forces under General William Howe, who would march north from New York City. To begin the invasion of the Champlain valley, Burgoyne had more than seven thousand men, nearly half of whom were German mercenaries, or soldiers who fought only for financial gain. Burgoyne also planned to send a force of about seven hundred regulars and loyalists under Colonel Barry St. Leger to attack American settlements and forts in the Mohawk River valley. These forces would be joined by nearly one thousand Iroquois Indians, who were native to this part of New York and were loyal to the British.

Though the area around Fort Ticonderoga had been fortified with artillery positions on nearby Mount Independence and Mount Hope, nothing had been done to strengthen Mount Defiance, as the Americans believed the steep slopes were too rugged to transport cannons. Burgoyne's military engineers, however, were able to fortify it, and when British artillery began shelling the Americans at the fort, General Arthur St. Clair realized the Americans had no choice but to retreat. On July 6, the Continental army headed south, and the British captured Fort Ticonderoga without a fight.

At Washington's request, Arnold joined General Schuyler at Fort Edward, north of Albany, New York, on July 22, 1777. His orders were to help Schuyler organize the defenses of the Northern Department. Nearly two

After fighting in the French and Indian War and earning the rank of major, Philip Schuyler became a member of the New York Assembly and a delegate to the Second Continental Congress. At the start of the American Revolution, Schuyler was made a general in the Continental army. This 1881 painting by Jacob Lazarus was based on an earlier portrait by John Trumbull.

thousand of Schuyler's six thousand men were sick, and many others lacked food and ammunition. Fortunately for the Americans, Burgoyne took his time moving forward and stopped at Skenesborough, New York, for nearly three weeks.

Arnold recruited more militia and helped to organize the American effort to slow Burgoyne's advance. On August 8, General Schuyler learned that St. Leger's forces were in the Mohawk valley and had begun a siege of Fort Stanwix in New York. Schuyler held a council of war, and the officers debated whether he should weaken his forces in front of Burgoyne in an effort to stop St. Leger. Schuyler approved this plan, which Arnold agreed to command.

Arnold led a column of about one thousand men to within striking distance of Fort Stanwix in just one week. He was eager to attack St. Leger at once. Some of his officers disagreed because Oneida Indian scouts, friendly to the Americans, reported that the enemy force was nearly twice as strong. At this point, a stroke of luck befell Arnold in the person of Hon Yost Schuyler.

Hon Yost Schuyler was a loyalist who had been captured by local militia and sentenced to death for helping to recruit soldiers for St. Leger. Schuyler's family came to Arnold's camp and made a plea for his life. They offered to send Hon Yost into the camp of St. Leger's Mohawk Indians and spread rumors of Arnold's overwhelming strength. Hon Yost had lived among these Indians and had a reputation for being a prophet from the Great Spirit who could see the future.

Arnold, sensing that the young man was truthful, gave him permission to enter the camp, but sent him with a trusted Oneida scout and held his mother and brother as hostages. When the two men reached the Mohawk camp, Hon Yost put on quite a performance. He claimed that the famous General Arnold was on his way with men as numerous as the leaves on the trees. The Mohawks, fearful of a long siege and aware of Arnold's reputation as a fierce fighter, broke camp to head back to their villages. Colonel St. Leger was unable to stop them and, with the number of his forces halved, retreated. On August 24, Arnold marched into Fort Stanwix. The threat to the Mohawk valley was over, and Arnold rejoined the American forces in front of Burgoyne.

While Arnold was marching west toward Fort Stanwix, General Gates had replaced General Schuyler as commander of the Northern Department. Congress held Schuyler responsible for the loss of Fort Ticonderoga, and Gates had been actively lobbying for the command. Although Arnold and Gates had worked well together in previous campaigns, their relationship in the months to come would be marked by jealousy. Schuyler had a high opinion of Arnold and was quick to praise him. Gates, however, saw himself as the savior of the Northern Department and had no wish for Arnold to upstage him.

When Arnold returned to army headquarters in Stillwater, New York, on August 30, Gates appointed him to command the left wing of Gate's army. Both men agreed that the American position had improved. General John Stark's militia had all but destroyed Burgoyne's force of 1,300 German mercenaries at the Battle of Bennington in Vermont. They could not agree, however, on a strategy to defeat Burgoyne. Arnold, always aggressive, wanted to attack. The more cautious Gates wanted to set up a strong defensive position and let Burgoyne attack him.

Arnold came up with another idea. At the advice of Colonel Thaddeus Kosciuszko, a Polish military engineer serving with the Continental army, Arnold suggested fortifying the high ground at Bemis Heights, which overlooked the Hudson River near Saratoga, New York. From there the patriots would command the road along the river, which Burgoyne had to use to march his army south toward Albany, forcing Burgoyne to attack. General Gates agreed to Arnold's plan, and Colonel Kosciuszko immediately supervised the construction of strong, earthwork fortifications. Behind these, some eight thousand Americans took their positions.

On September 19, General Burgoyne prepared for an attack against the American lines. When American scouts reported the British advance, Arnold wanted to attack near the woods at Freeman's Farm, just in front of Bemis Heights. Gates reluctantly permitted Arnold to move

ahead. Arnold's soldiers almost won the day during several hours of fighting, but, lacking reinforcements at a critical time, had to withdraw at nightfall. The British remained in control of Freeman's Farm, but had lost more than five hundred men.

After the battle at Freeman's Farm, Arnold urged Gates to attack before Burgoyne's army had a chance to fortify their position. Gates refused and further angered Arnold by sending a report to Congress that made no mention of Arnold or the key officers who had fought with him. After an argument at Gates's headquarters on September 22, Arnold demanded a pass to Philadelphia to join Washington. Arnold's officers urged him to remain, and he agreed to stay. He had no command, however, as Gates took charge of his regiments.

General Burgoyne's position was desperate. His supply line to Fort Ticonderoga was increasingly vulnerable to American raids, and his army was dwindling. When he realized that reinforcements would not arrive, Burgoyne had to decide whether to retreat or fight. He decided on another attack. On the morning of October 7, he personally led 1,500 men to test the American lines for a weak spot. As his soldiers approached the clearing of another farm, the Barber Farm, American scouts reported his advance to General Gates, who ordered an attack.

Previous spread: This drawing of General Burgoyne's surrender to the Continental forces at Saratoga was created by François Godefroy in Paris around 1783.

During the next several hours of fighting, Benedict Arnold appeared. Though he had no official command, he couldn't sit quietly in his tent. As he galloped onto the field, many of his men gave a wild cheer, and Arnold took charge of a second assault on the center of Burgoyne's line, which broke and fell back to the defensive redoubts on Freeman's Farm. Arnold continued his pursuit. When Arnold's men reached a redoubt held by Colonel Heinrich Breymann's Germans, Arnold galloped to the front, pointed his sword, and charged. As Arnold spurred his horse into the redoubt, a German volley killed his horse and another musket shot slammed into his left leg. Falling critically wounded, he urged his men to "Rush On!" and the German defenders fled.

Burgoyne, realizing he was defeated, withdrew from Freeman's Farm that night. The following day his entire army retreated 5 miles (8 km) upriver to Saratoga. With his army all but surrounded and no hope of reinforcements, Burgoyne agreed to surrender on October 17. Gates soon received the official thanks of Congress for the victory and was celebrated as the Hero of Saratoga. General Burgoyne saw the matter differently, however. He observed in a letter to General Sir Henry Clinton that the defeat "was his [Arnold's] doing."

7. Military Governor of Philadelphia

Arnold never fully recovered from his leg wound. For the rest of his life he wore a special shoe with a built-up heel, and he would often use a crutch or a cane when he walked. He spent several months in a hospital in Albany, where he was not a good patient. In March 1778, he returned to Connecticut and visited with his family. General Washington wrote to him during his recovery, expressing concern and his hope that Arnold could soon return to duty. On May 21, 1778, Arnold rejoined Washington at his camp at Valley Forge, Pennsylvania, and on May 30 he took the oath of allegiance to the United States, which was a requirement for all officers.

Washington knew that Arnold was eager for another command. Concerned about Arnold's health, Washington offered him the position of military governor of Philadelphia. The British army had occupied the city since September 1777, and as General Howe was preparing to evacuate his forces from Philadelphia to New York, the Continental Congress and the Supreme Executive Council of Pennsylvania could return. It

By signing this oath of allegiance to the United States of America on May 30, 1778, Benedict Arnold was pledging his loyalty to the new nation. This signed document also stated that Arnold would not obey George III of Great Britain.

would be Arnold's job to maintain order and enforce the law.

Arnold arrived in Philadelphia on June 19, 1778. The British had been careful to protect many of the brick townhouses and shops of the city's wealthy Quakers and loyalists near the waterfront, but much of the city had been destroyed. Arnold observed blocks of buildings and fences that had been torn down for firewood. In present-day Washington Square, Arnold was shocked to find that the bodies of nearly two thousand American prisoners of war who had died the previous winter had been dumped into large trench graves.

Congress learned that some loyalist merchants were planning to hide their goods, then sell them at much

Back of the State House, Philadelphia, was published by William Birch and Sons in 1799. Christ Church, the building at the center of this engraving, was constructed between 1727 and 1744. The tall steeple dominated the city's skyline. The patriots George Washington, Benjamin Franklin, and Betsy Ross all came here to worship.

higher prices when the Americans reoccupied the city. Arnold received orders to stop the "removal, transfer or sale of any goods, wares or merchandise in possession of the inhabitants." Arnold was to close all businesses until further notice and prevent looting.

As soon as Arnold published these orders and closed the shops, he was blamed for unfair treatment. Many patriot merchants had expected that only the loyalists would be punished. As time passed, a number of the city's residents came to dislike Arnold's rich lifestyle. He established his headquarters in the Penn Mansion, which until recently had been British general Howe's headquarters. Arnold filled his residence with expensive furniture. His sister Hannah came from New Haven, and she helped him to arrange dinner parties for some of the city's wealthiest families, including suspected loyalists.

To support his expensive lifestyle, Arnold used his authority to engage in controversial business deals. It wasn't unusual in the 1700s for officers to take advantage of their positions. Arnold entered into a partnership with the clothier general of the Continental army to split the profits from the sale of British army surplus goods that were left behind. Earlier, Arnold had also given a pass to ship owner Robert Shewell so that he could sail his schooner the *Charming Nancy* out of the city to trade with other American ports. Though Arnold had issued this pass before Congress had enacted a law prohibiting all goods from leaving the city, some residents were convinced that he was granting special favors.

Not long after, the *Charming Nancy* was captured by an American privateer and was taken into Egg Harbor, New Jersey. Though the ship was released, word reached Arnold that the British were threatening to seize all the shipping that came into Egg Harbor, prompting him to send twelve government wagons to unload the ship's cargo and bring it back to Philadelphia. There the cargo was sold, and Arnold shared the profits with Shewell. This misuse of government property would come back to haunt Arnold in a few months.

In the summer of 1778, as Arnold settled into his command, he became a regular visitor at the mansion of Edward Shippen. The Shippens were one of the city's wealthiest families. Although members of his family served in the Continental army, many in the city suspected that Edward was a loyalist, for he had entertained General Howe and his officers during the British occupation. The real attraction in the Shippen house, however, was his three daughters. Arnold was especially drawn to eighteen-year-old Margaret, known as Peggy, as was Arnold's first wife. Many British officers had courted her, including John André, a handsome, twenty-six-year-old aide to General Charles Grey. André had a love of poetry, art, and the theater and had helped to organize several plays at the Southwark theater to entertain General Howe and his guests.

Over the coming months, Arnold courted Peggy. One of Arnold's friends, Mrs. Robert Morris, remarked in a letter that "Cupid has given our little general a more mortal wound, than all the host of Britons could—Miss Peggy Shippen is the fair one." Edward Shippen first opposed the match, but he eventually changed his mind, and in the spring of 1779, the couple married.

Though Arnold was successful in love, he was in serious trouble with the Pennsylvania authorities and with Congress. Joseph Reed, soon to become the president of the Supreme Executive Council of Pennsylvania, disliked Arnold and did not care for the manner in which Arnold

John André drew this pencil sketch of Margaret "Peggy" Shippen in 1778. Peggy frequently attended theatrical productions at the Southwark Playhouse, where André acted in minor roles and designed sets. André did many sketches of Peggy, and the two would spend hours discussing the latest play at the Southwark.

favored loyalists. Determined to see Arnold removed from his post, Reed and the Pennsylvania Council issued charges against him in February 1779, and instructed the state's attorney general to indict Arnold. The charges included accusations that he had granted an illegal pass to allow the *Charming Nancy* to leave the city, had used public wagons to transport private goods, and had issued illegal passes for loyalists to travel to British-occupied New York.

When Arnold learned of these charges, he went to General Washington's headquarters in New Jersey. Washington urged him to return to Philadelphia to defend himself. On February 16, Congress voted to have the charges evaluated by a special committee. On March 5, Arnold defended himself before the Committee, which cleared him of all but two charges, those of using government property to haul private goods, and "abuse of the militia" for personal reasons. The Committee recommended that these charges be handled by a military court-martial, and not by a public trial. Arnold, satisfied with this, resigned his position as military governor.

News of the Committee report angered Reed and the Pennsylvania delegation, which demanded further investigation. In a compromise with Reed, Congress reinstated more of the charges, then ordered them all turned over to General Washington for a court-martial. Washington, clearly sympathetic to Arnold, wrote Arnold a letter promising a court-martial by May 1.

Reed was still not satisfied and sought to gather more evidence against Arnold. In a letter to Washington on April 24, Reed requested that the court-martial be delayed and threatened to use his power to withhold badly needed wagons for Washington's army if the commanding general did not agree. Not wishing to defy the entire Pennsylvania Congressional delegation, Washington reluctantly agreed. He advised Arnold in a letter that the court-martial would have to be postponed. Arnold was upset, and, in a desperate letter to Washington, pleaded for quick action:

> *Having made every sacrifice of fortune and blood, and become a cripple in the service of my country, I little expected to meet the ungrateful returns I have received from my countrymen . . . I have nothing left but the little reputation I have gained in the army. Delay in the present case is worse than death.*

Even as he wrote this letter, Arnold had begun thinking that perhaps all his sacrifices for the American cause would never be appreciated. He was angry with Congress, which had so often questioned his honesty and conduct. He concluded that perhaps the United States was no longer worth fighting for. In May 1779, Arnold made up his mind to approach the British to see what they would offer him for changing his allegiance.

8. Treason at West Point

Long after the British evacuated Philadelphia, Peggy Arnold and her friends continued writing to John André, then serving as an aide to General Henry Clinton in New York. Though historians are not certain, some believe that Peggy asked André which person in Philadelphia could be trusted to carry a secret message to General Clinton. André recommended a merchant named Joseph Stansbury. In early May 1779, Benedict Arnold invited Stansbury to a meeting at his house. He told Stansbury "under a solemn obligation of secrecy, his intention of opening his services to the commander-in-chief of the British forces." Stansbury delivered the message to André in New York on May 10.

In his written response, André told Arnold that General Clinton had a sincere interest in his offer. He suggested that Arnold could be of greatest service to the British by passing along important military information. He also instructed Arnold to write future letters in a secret code, hidden by invisible ink between the lines of an otherwise normal-looking letter from his wife Peggy or one of her friends. The code would be based on a book called *Blackstone's Commentaries on the Laws of England*, which both men would own. To create the code, each word of the message would consist of three numbers. The first number would tell the reader which page to look for, and the second and third numbers would indicate what line and word should be read on that page. Unless another reader had access to the same book, the code would be impossible to break.

Over the next several months, Arnold continued to negotiate the terms of his services, even as he offered information about Washington's army as a show of good faith. On July 11, 1779, Joseph Stansbury delivered a message to André from Arnold that gave General Clinton the first idea of how much money Arnold wanted up front as payment for his defection:

> *He expects to have your promise that he shall be indemnified for any loss he may sustain in case of detection, and, whether this contest is finished by sword or treaty, that 10,000 pounds shall be engaged to him for his services.*

Major André replied that the British could not guarantee so much money unless Arnold could deliver something important. Since Arnold did not have a command, the formal negotiations between the two parties broke off, and did not start again for almost another year.

This is the second page of a coded letter sent by Arnold to André on July 12, 1780. Benedict Arnold gave the British crucial knowledge in this letter regarding the movement of American and French forces, information that Arnold received from George Washington, commander of the Continental army. Arnold told the British that he would soon become commander at West Point, a position that would make him privileged to essential information.

Even as he considered treason, Arnold still hoped to clear the charges brought against him by Joseph Reed. The long-awaited court-martial began at Washington's headquarters in Morristown, New Jersey, in late December 1779. The court acquitted Arnold of any intentional wrongdoing, but it still directed the commanding general to issue him a formal reprimand. In his letter to Arnold, Washington expressed his disappointment at his behavior, noting, "even the shadow of a fault tarnishes the lustre of our finest achievements."

For someone as sensitive as Arnold, Washington's letter amounted to a complete show of no confidence. If his best ally no longer held him in high esteem, what further reason was there for him to continue fighting for the American cause? Arnold had few doubts about his wish to change sides, but he needed the right opportunity to make his offer attractive to the British. He set his sights on the command at West Point, New York.

Called the key to America by George Washington, the forts at West Point were located on high bluffs overlooking a point where the Hudson River makes two ninety-degree turns. Enemy ships sailing past would be vulnerable, as they would have to slow down through the narrow passage and could not elevate their cannons high enough to fire back at the defenders. Control of West Point assured the Americans access to the

Hudson River, a vital link between New England and the middle Atlantic and southern states.

Arnold saw his opportunity in April 1780, when his friend General Schuyler, then a New York delegate to Congress, became chairman of a congressional committee charged with exploring the reorganization of the army. Schuyler and another politician, Robert Livingston, agreed to approach Washington about the West Point command. Schuyler advised Arnold by letter on June 2 that he believed Washington would give him his choice of assignments.

Arnold resumed his correspondence with André, and in a letter dated July 15, 1780, asked him: "If I point out a plan of co-operation by which Sir Henry Clinton shall possess himself of West Point, the Garrison, etc., etc., etc., twenty thousand pounds sterling I think will be a cheap purchase for an object of so much importance." John André replied on July 24 that "Should we through your means possess ourselves of 3000 men and its [West Point's] artillery and stores . . . the sum even of 20,000 pounds should be paid you." Transporting André's message through the American lines was difficult, and by the time Peggy Arnold passed the letter to her husband, Arnold had taken command of West Point.

Arnold needed a plan to weaken the defenses of West Point without creating suspicion, and to arrange the time and place when the British would attack and capture the forts. After two unsuccessful attempts to meet André at

Dobbs Ferry on September 11 and 20, Arnold suggested that André come to West Point disguised as a merchant. On the evening of September 21, Joshua Hett Smith, an agent whom Arnold had recruited, boarded the British ship *Vulture* near Teller's Point. Here he was instructed to escort "Mr. John Anderson" to a nighttime meeting with Arnold in the nearby woods. When that meeting concluded, it was too late to make it back to the *Vulture* in darkness, so Smith and Arnold escorted John André to Smith's house about 4 miles (6.4 km) away.

The next morning, Arnold was horrified to find that the *Vulture* had been driven downstream by American artillery fire from Teller's Point. André, who had never intended to go deep behind enemy lines in disguise, was in trouble. He reluctantly agreed to Arnold's plan to carry the papers detailing the defenses of West Point and to use Joshua Hett Smith as a guide to lead him overland back to the British lines near Dobbs Ferry. The two men left Smith's house and headed north toward Stony Point. They traveled through the American lines with safe conduct passes provided by Arnold.

Joshua Hett Smith and John André traveled together as far as Pine's Bridge on the Croton River. From there André went ahead on his own. He had gotten as far as Tarrytown when a band of local men stopped him. André, thinking that the men were loyalists, made the mistake of identifying himself as a British officer. The men searched him and found the documents hidden under his

This safe-conduct pass was written on September 21, 1780, by Benedict Arnold. The pass allowed Joshua Hett Smith and several other men to travel to Dobbs Ferry.

socks. They took John André prisoner and turned him over to Colonel John Jameson's command at North Castle.

Information of John André's capture reached Arnold at his headquarters at Robinson House on the morning of September 25, 1780. Colonel Jameson had forwarded the captured papers to General Washington, who was scheduled to visit Arnold for breakfast that morning. Realizing that as soon as Washington looked at the documents he would recognize Arnold's treason, Arnold calmly informed Peggy of the news. He gave his aide David Franks an excuse that he had been called away on urgent business and galloped down the river to escape on his private barge. Within a few hours, Arnold's barge had taken him to the *Vulture*.

Washington and his staff arrived at Robinson House about 10:30 A.M., and at first were not alarmed at Arnold's absence. When Colonel Jameson's messenger arrived with the captured documents, Washington ordered his aides Alexander Hamilton and James McHenry to catch the traitor. The distressed commander in chief commented, "Arnold has betrayed me. Whom can we trust now?"

After Arnold boarded the *Vulture*, he wrote a letter to Washington, which reached the general later that afternoon. In it Arnold used the opportunity to explain his actions:

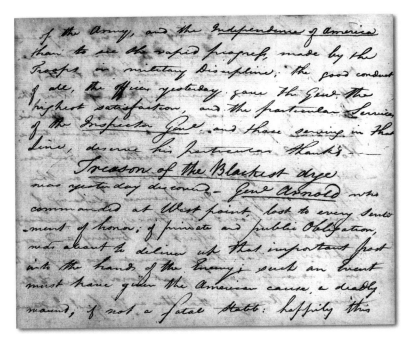

The West Point Officer of the Watch wrote this entry in the orderly book, or official diary, in September 1780, the day after Arnold's treason was discovered. He wrote: "Treason of the Blackest dye was yesterday discovered . . . [had Arnold succeeded, it would have given] the American cause a deadly wound. . . ."

I have ever acted from a principle of love to my country, since the commencement of the present unhappy contest between Great Britain and the Colonies. The same principle of love to my country actuates my present conduct, however it may appear inconsistent to the world, who very seldom judge right of any man's actions.

Arnold also asked that his wife Peggy not be blamed for any role in his treason, as she was "as good and as innocent as an angel." Arnold assured Washington that his aides knew nothing of his plans.

Though Washington was unable to capture Arnold, Major John André was being held prisoner at Mabie's Tavern in Tappan, New York. Washington ordered a board of his high-ranking officers to hold a trial and recommend punishment. On September 29, the trial board met at the Dutch church in Tappan with General Nathanael Greene as president and thirteen other officers.

The key issue of the trial was whether or not André should be treated as a captured spy or as a prisoner of war. The strongest evidence against André came from his own testimony and from a letter he had written to General Washington. In both cases, he admitted that he had traveled behind American lines in disguise and had carried important military documents hidden in his boots. When General Greene asked André if he believed he had operated under the protection of a flag of truce, André reportedly replied, "it was impossible for him to suppose he came on shore under that sanction, and added that if he came on shore under that sanction he certainly might have returned under it."

After the board finished questioning André, they dismissed him in order to discuss letters sent by General Henry Clinton and Benedict Arnold. Both men argued that André had indeed come ashore under a flag of truce and had acted under Arnold's orders while behind

This is a self-portrait created by John André. The sketch was drawn at Mabie's Tavern at Tappan on October 1, 1780, the day before André's execution. Eyewitnesses said that George Washington's hand shook with emotion when he signed the warrant for André's execution.

American lines, and therefore could not be considered a spy. After reviewing these letters, however, General Greene and his officers concluded that André had "come on shore in a private and secret manner," that he had "changed his dress within our lines," and had attempted to carry back to the British "several papers which contained intelligence for the enemy." The board then passed sentence, and all the officers signed the following statement that was forwarded to General Washington:

> That Major André, adjutant general to the British army, ought to be considered as a spy from the enemy; and that, agreeable to the law and usage of nations, it is their opinion he ought to suffer death.

On September 30, Washington posted orders for André's execution. Throughout André's imprisonment and trial, he had impressed the Americans with his strength of character, honesty, and courage. Many felt that the wrong person was being tried, and, in the next few days, both sides tried to negotiate a deal. General Clinton sought André's release, while the Americans hinted that if Arnold were sent back, André would be freed. All of these efforts failed. On Tuesday, October 2, 1780, André was escorted from Mabie's Tavern to a field about ¼ mile (.4 km) away, where a gallows had been erected.

André stepped onto a wagon underneath the gallows, which would support his body until the moment of execution. John André took the rope from his executioner and adjusted the noose around his own neck. In the words of one patriot official, "he then took from his coat pocket a white silk handkerchief and tied it over his own eyes. The perfect firmness with which he acted melted our hearts." When the officer in charge of the execution, Colonel Alexander Scammel, asked if he had any final words, André raised the handkerchief from his eyes and said "I pray you to bear witness that I met my fate like a brave man." Many in the crowd wept as the wagon pulled away.

André was buried next to the gallows. Forty-one years later, his remains were moved to Westminster Abbey in London, England. *The Unfortunate Death of Major John André*, a 1783 engraving by Goldar, was based on a painting by Hamilton.

9. Benedict Arnold, British General

As news of Arnold's treason spread around the country, Americans made a public display of their anger. In Norwich, a mob rushed into the cemetery and destroyed the gravestones of his father and infant brother because they bore the name Benedict Arnold.

When Peggy Arnold returned to Philadelphia from West Point to be with her family, the Supreme Executive Council ordered her to leave within two weeks, never to be allowed to return. Perhaps Benjamin Franklin best expressed the feelings of his countrymen toward Arnold when he wrote, "Judas sold only one man, Arnold three millions."

If most Americans hated Arnold, he was little loved by his new allies in New York. Though General Henry Clinton received him with great courtesy, many British officers blamed him for the death of their friend John André. These feelings stiffened Arnold's resolve to prove his value to the British. Already he had proven to himself that treason could be profitable. In addition to his commission as a brigadier general in the British army, Arnold

This woodcut depicts a two-faced effigy of Benedict Arnold with the devil standing behind him. The effigy is carried on a cart through the streets of Philadelphia to be burned by an angry mob.

was awarded 6,000 pounds, a lifetime pension for his children, and commissions in the British army for his sons when they were old enough to serve.

In December 1780, General Clinton agreed to let Arnold lead a raid against American supplies and shipping on the James River in Virginia. After landing near Williamsburg, Virginia, on January 4, 1781, Arnold's column marched toward the new state capital of Richmond. Here the British set fire to warehouses full of tobacco and other merchandise. Arnold also destroyed the warehouses, the mills, and the clothing depot at Chesterfield before marching to Portsmouth. Though Arnold had some hopes that he might command a large scale British operation in

Virginia or North Carolina, those hopes were dashed when Lord Charles Cornwallis arrived in Portsmouth in May. Arnold was ordered to return to New York.

At the end of August, General Clinton allowed Arnold to lead a raid on New London, Connecticut. This vital Connecticut seaport had provided safe harbor for American privateers that had captured many British merchant ships and was also an important depot for Continental supplies.

Arnold left New York with a fleet of 24 ships and 1,700 men and landed his forces on both sides of New London harbor on the morning of September 6. One column of eight hundred men led by Arnold himself moved toward the town of New London. The other column, led by Lieutenant Colonel Edmund Eyre, moved toward the village of Groton to attack Fort Griswold, which protected the harbor. In New London, the local militia were poorly organized and put up little resistance. Arnold's men easily captured Fort Trumbull and Town Hill Fort, and then set fire to the ships and warehouses along the Thames River. The fires spread, and soon much of the town was ablaze.

Across the river, in Groton, British units met heavy resistance at Fort Griswold, where a small group of volunteers and local militia put up a stiff fight. Twice the British attackers were driven back with heavy losses. On the third assault, the British finally broke through the main gate. The American commander Colonel William

Ledyard and more than eighty of his men were killed after Ledyard had surrendered. Unfortunately, some of Ledyard's men had not known of the surrender and had continued firing, and the British had responded with additional volleys. This led the Americans to charge later that the British had committed cold-blooded murder. Local residents would ever after refer to the British forces as Traitor Arnold's Murdering Corps.

Arnold's New London raid proved to be his last British command. A month later Lord Cornwallis surrendered his army to French and American forces at Yorktown, Virginia, all but ending the American Revolution.

10. Last Years in Canada and England

While many British officers viewed the end of the war as certain, Arnold was not ready to give up. With the permission of Sir Henry Clinton, he sailed with Peggy for London in December 1781. Arnold hoped to convince King George and his ministers that a large number of loyalists wanted to continue the fight, and that with more British reinforcements, they could still win. The Arnolds arrived in London on January 22, 1782. They rented a house on Portman Square, close to the homes of many loyalists who had immigrated to England.

During the next weeks, Arnold visited the king's ministers. All listened to his arguments and expressed interest. King George and Queen Charlotte both gave the Arnolds a warm reception and permitted him to address King George's privy council. However successful these meetings were, they did little for Arnold's military hopes. The growing antiwar feeling among members of Parliament soon resulted in a change of political power, and the pro-war ministers were forced to resign.

Although Arnold's hopes of achieving another military command were probably dim, he was not about to remain idle. Moreover, his family was growing. In addition to his three sons, who still lived with his sister Hannah in New Haven, his wife Peggy bore five children between 1780 and 1785. While two of these children died in infancy, two sons and a daughter would survive to adulthood. As did many other loyalists, Arnold looked to a possible future in Canada. After the Treaty of Paris, signed in 1783, officially granted American independence, thousands of loyalists fled to Canada. As Arnold saw it, the large influx of settlers provided a wonderful business opportunity to sell goods purchased in England. Scraping together enough funds to purchase a ship called the *Lord Middlebrook*, Arnold sailed for Canada in October 1785.

After some initial difficulties, Arnold settled in Saint John, New Brunswick. He established a successful business and built a handsome mansion on King Street. Peggy came from London to join him, and Hannah moved from New Haven with Arnold's three older sons. His family was together for the first time, and it appeared that Arnold might have the business success and domestic comforts that had so long escaped him. Like so much else in his turbulent life, this serenity did not last. Arnold's prosperity was hampered by the breakup of a partnership he had formed with Munson Hayt, a former loyalist officer who had served under him. When Arnold tried to collect the

BY
Brigadier-General ARNOLD,
A PROCLAMATION.

To the Officers and Soldiers of the Continental Army who have the real
Interest of their Country at Heart, and who are determined to be
no longer the Tools and Dupes of Congress, or of France.

HAVING reafon to believe that the principles I have avowed, in my addrefs to the public of the 7th inftant, animated the greateft part of this continent, I rejoice in the opportunity I have of inviting you to join His Majefty's Arms.

His Excellency Sir *Henry Clinton* has authorized me to raife a corps of cavalry and infantry, who are to be clothed, fubfifted, and paid as the other troops are in the Britifh fervice, and thofe who bring in horfes, arms, or accoutrements, are to be paid their value, or have liberty to fell them: To every non-commiffioned officer and private a bounty of THREE GUINEAS will be given, and as the Commander in Chief is pleafed to allow me to nominate the officers, I fhall with infinite fatisfaction embrace this opportunity of advancing men whofe valour I have witneffed, and whofe principles are favourable to an union with *Britain*, and TRUE AMERICAN LIBERTY.

The rank they obtain in the King's fervice will bear a proportion to their former rank, and the number of men they bring with them.

It is expected that a Lieutenant-Colonel of cavalry will bring with him, or recruit in a reafonable time, 75 men,

Major of *HORSE* - 50 men.	Lieut. Col. of *INFANTRY* - 75 men.
Captain of ditto - - - 30	Major of ditto - - - - - - - - - 50
Lieutenant of ditto - 15	Captain of ditto - - - - - - - 30
Cornet of ditto - - - 12	Lieutenant of ditto - - - - - - 15
Serjeant of ditto - - - 6	Enfign of ditto - - - - - - - - 12
	Serjeant of ditto - - - - - - - 6

N. B. Each Field Officer will have a Company.

Great as this encouragement muft appear to fuch as have fuffered every diftrefs of want of pay, hunger and nakednefs, from the neglect, contempt, and corruption of Congrefs, they are nothing to the motives which I expect will influence the brave and generous minds I hope to have the honour to command.

I wifh to lead a chofen band of Americans to the attainment of peace, liberty, and fafety (that firft object in taking the field) and with them to fhare in the glory of refcuing our native country from the grafping hand of *France*, as well as from the ambitious and interefted views of a defperate party among ourfelves, who, in liftening to *French* overtures, and rejecting thofe from *Great-Britain*, have brought the colonies to the very brink of deftruction.

Friends, fellow foldiers, and citizens, aroufe, and judge for yourfelves,—reflect on what you have loft,—confider to what you are reduced, and by your courage repel the ruin that ftill threatens you.

Your country once was happy, and had the proffered peace been embraced, your laft two years of mifery had been fpent in peace and plenty, and repairing the defolations of a quarrel that would have fet the intereft of *Great-Britain* and *America* in its true light, and cemented their friendfhip; whereas, you are now the prey of avarice, the fcorn of your enemies, and the pity of your friends.

You were promifed LIBERTY by the leaders of your affairs; but is there an individual in the enjoyment of it, faving your oppreffors? Who among you dare fpeak, or write what he thinks, againft the tyranny which has robbed you of your property, imprifons your perfons, drags you to the field of battle, and is daily deluging your country with your blood?

You are flattered with independency as preferable to a redrefs of grievances, and for that fhadow, inftead . . . . rty by . . . . pacity of your own rulers. Already

Brigadier-General Benedict Arnold recruited soldiers from the Continental army in this 1780 broadside. Arnold reassured American officers that their rank in the British army would be similar to their rank in the Continental army if they met certain standards.

insurance on one of his warehouses, which burned in the summer of 1788, Hayt claimed that Arnold had deliberately set the fire. Arnold sued Hayt for slander, and although the jury found in his favor, the judge awarded him only a small fine. Many in Saint John sympathized with Hayt, and the news of the verdict prompted a mob to loot Arnold's house and burn an effigy of him in front of his home.

In the fall of 1791, Arnold and his family returned to England. During the next several years, Arnold resumed his trading activities in the West Indies, an area he knew well from his youth. When France and England went to war in 1793, Arnold offered his services to the British government. Though he was not granted a commission, he served as a volunteer and helped British plantation owners to end a slave revolt on the island of Guadeloupe. The independent command he had craved for so long still eluded him, and the death of his oldest son, Benedict, in 1796, caused him to despair. Over the objections of his father, the younger Benedict had joined the British army and was mortally wounded in combat in Jamaica.

In February 1801, just a month after he turned sixty, Arnold's health rapidly declined. In the words of biographer Willard Sterne Randall, "he did not seem to want to fight any longer." Arnold died in London on June 14, 1801. Two weeks later, in a letter to their son Edward, Peggy wrote:

For his own sake the change [death] is a most happy one, as the disappointment of all his expectations . . . had so broken his spirits and destroyed his nerves, that he has been for a long time past incapable of the smallest enjoyment.

Arnold's funeral took place on June 21, when his body was laid to rest in a crypt beneath St. Mary's

This memorial stained glass window (*left*) in St. Mary's Battersea Church in London honors Benedict Arnold, who is buried beneath the church's crypt. The memorial, dedicated in 1976, was commissioned by a U.S. citizen in honor of the American bicentennial. This plaque (*right*) adorns the Arnolds' crypt.

Church in London. His devoted wife Peggy joined him there just three years later, a victim of cancer at the age of forty-four.

Arnold's death prompted little notice in London newspapers, and even less in America. He died a man without a country, and to many people, a despised traitor. Some biographers tried to suggest that in his last moments, Arnold had felt sorry for all that he had done and had asked Peggy if he could try on his old Continental uniform once more. This story has no basis in fact.

It is more likely that Arnold believed he had been faithful to his personal sense of honor, and to his country, even if most people didn't agree. As he wrote to Washington not long after he boarded the *Vulture*, "The same principle of love to my country actuates my present conduct, however it may appear inconsistent to the world, who very seldom judge right of any man's actions."

Though most people still judge Arnold harshly, his legacy does not deserve to be forgotten. His descendants were important and productive citizens in England and Canada, and remain so today. Perhaps that, and the nation his victories helped to save, is what we should remember most about Benedict Arnold.

Timeline

1741	Benedict Arnold is born in Norwich, Connecticut.
1752	Benedict Arnold enrolls in Reverend James Cogswell's school.
1753	Benedict's sisters Mary and Elizabeth die in an epidemic.
1754	Benedict becomes an apprentice in the Lathrops' apothecary shop in Norwich.
1759	Arnold's mother, Hannah, dies.
1761	Arnold's father, Benedict, dies.
1762	Benedict opens a shop in New Haven, Connecticut.
1766	Benedict Arnold is indicted in the Peter Boles case.
1767	Arnold marries Margaret "Peggy" Mansfield in New Haven.
1775	Benedict Arnold leads an attack on Fort Ticonderoga with Ethan Allen.
	Peggy Arnold dies.
	Colonel Arnold leads his men through the Maine wilderness on the march to Quebec and is wounded while attacking the city.
1776	Arnold fights in the Battle of Valcour Island on Lake Champlain.
1777	Arnold fights in the Battle of Ridgefield.
	Arnold marches to save Fort Stanwix.
	Arnold is wounded in the Battle of Saratoga.

1778	Arnold becomes military governor of Philadelphia.
1779	Arnold marries Margaret "Peggy" Shippen.
	Arnold begins correspondence with the British.
1780	Arnold defects to the British after trying to turn over West Point.
1781	Benedict Arnold raids New London, Connecticut.
	Benedict and Peggy move to London.
1787	The Arnold family settles in Saint John, New Brunswick, Canada.
1791	The Arnolds return to London.
1793	Arnold serves as a volunteer, fighting in the West Indies.
1796	Arnold's oldest son, Benedict, is killed in combat.
1801	Benedict Arnold dies in London and is buried at St. Mary's Church, Battersea.

Glossary

apprentice (uh-PREN-tis) An individual who works without pay in order to learn a skill or a craft.

barracks (BAR-iks) A building or a group of buildings used to house soldiers.

barricade (BAR-uh-kayd) A structure set up to stop the passage of an enemy.

bateau (ba-TOH) A flat-bottomed boat that usually has flared sides.

battalions (buh-TAL-yunz) Large groups of soldiers organized as units, usually made up of two or more companies.

Continental Congress (kon-tin-EN-tul KON-gres) A political body that directed the American Revolution.

court-martial (KORT-mar-shul) A trial held under military, not civillian, authority.

defection (dih-FEK-shun) The giving up of one's loyalty to one group or country to join another.

descendants (dih-SEN-dents) People who are born from a certain family or group.

effigy (EH-fuh-jee) A crude figure or dummy that represents a hated person.

flagship (FLAG-ship) A ship that carries the commander of a group of ships and that flies his or her flag.

flanking (FLANK-ing) Attacking the right or left side of a fort or a line of soldiers.

galley (GA-lee) A long, narrow ship that moves by use of oars.

gallows (GA-lohz) A structure by which a person is executed by hanging.

garrison (GAR-ih-sun) The troops stationed at a fort or other military posts.

Georgian style (JOR-jun STYL) A style of building named for the Georges, kings of Great Britain during the colonial period.

indictment (in-DYT-ment) A written statement issued by a grand jury that charges a person with a crime.

lobbying (LAH-bee-ing) Attempting to influence someone to do something.

looting (LOOT-ing) Taking or stealing goods, sometimes by using violence.

loyalists (LOY-uh-lists) People who remained loyal to the British Crown during the American Revolution.

miscreants (MIS-kree-unts) People who behave horribly or criminally.

Parliament (PAR-lih-mint) The national legislature of Britain, made up of the House of Commons and the House of Lords.

privateer (pry-vuh-TEER) A ship that is privately owned but given permission by a country to attack enemy ships in time of war.

redoubts (ri-DOWTS) Temporary fortifications used to secure hilltops, passes, or the flanks of entrenchments.

reinforcements (re-in-FORS-ments) Additional soldiers sent to help an army or to help defend a fort.

routed (ROWT-ed) Badly defeated and forced to retreat quickly.

schooner (SKOO-ner) A fast, sturdy boat with two masts.

sentry (SEN-tree) A guard, especially a soldier, posted at a given spot to prevent the passage of unwanted people or soldiers.

serenity (suh-REH-nih-tee) A feeling of calm or peacefulness.

shipwrights (SHIP-ryts) Craftspeople or carpenters who specialize in building ships.

sloops (SLOOPS) Ships with one mast and with sails in the front and back.

Additional Resources

To learn more about Benedict Arnold and his times, check out these books and Web sites:

Books

Fritz, Jean. *Traitor: The Case of Benedict Arnold*. New York: Putnam and Grosset Group, 1997.

Roberts, Kenneth. *Rabble in Arms*. Camden, ME: Down East Books, 1996.

Web Sites

Due to the changing nature of Internet links, PowerPlus Books has developed an online list of Web sites related to the subject of this book. This site is updated regularly. Please use this link to access the list:
www.powerkidslinks.com/lalt/barnold/

Bibliography

Arnold, Isaac N. *The Life of Benedict Arnold: His Patriotism and His Treason*. Chicago: Jansen, McClurg and Company, 1880.

Bailey, Anthony. *Major André*. New York: Farrar, Straus, Giroux, 1987.

Caulkins, Frances M. *History of Norwich, Connecticut*. Norwich, CT: T. Robinson, 1845.

Flexner, James Thomas. *The Traitor and the Spy: Benedict Arnold and John André*. Boston: Little, Brown and Company, 1975.

Lundeberg, Philip K. *The Gunboat* Philadelphia *and the Defense of Lake Champlain in 1776*. Basin Harbor, VT: Lake Champlain Maritime Museum, 1995.

Martin, James Kirby. *Benedict Arnold, Revolutionary Hero*. New York: New York University Press, 1997.

Pell, Stephen H. P. *Fort Ticonderoga*. Fort Ticonderoga, NY: Fort Ticonderoga Museum, 1968.

Powell, Walter L. *Murder or Mayhem? Benedict Arnold's New London, Connecticut Raid, 1781*. Gettysburg, PA: Thomas Publications, 2000.

Randall, Willard Sterne. *Benedict Arnold: Patriot and Traitor*. New York: William Morrow and Company, 1990.

Roberts, Kenneth. *March to Quebec*. New York: Doubleday, Doran and Company, Inc., 1938.

Sparks, Jared. *The Life and Treason of Benedict Arnold*. Boston: Hilliard, Gray, 1835

Taylor, J. G. *Some New Light on the Later Life and Last Resting Place of Benedict Arnold and of His Wife Margaret Shippen*. Chelsea, London: George White, 1931.

Van Doren, Carl. *Secret History of the American Revolution*. New York: The Viking Press, 1941.

Wallace, Willard M. *Appeal to Arms: A Military History of the American Revolution.* New York: Harper and Brothers, 1951.

Wallace, Willard M. *Traitorous Hero: The Life and Fortunes of Benedict Arnold.* New York: Harper and Brothers, 1954.

Index

About the Author

Dr. Walter L. Powell is the historic preservation officer for the Borough of Gettysburg. He has lectured and written widely on the subjects of the American Revolution and the Civil War and is a specialist in seventeenth- and eighteenth-century New England history. He is currently president of the Braddock Road Preservation Association. Dr. Powell is a former licensed battlefield guide at the Gettysburg National Military Park and the past president of the Gettysburg Battlefield Preservation Association. Dr. Powell has written several articles for the *Connecticut Historical Society Bulletin* and was the editor of the book *Connecticut Yankees at Gettysburg*, which was published by Kent State University Press in 1993.

Primary Sources

Cover. *Colonel Benedict Arnold*, mezzotint, 1776, Corbutt, Anne S. K. Brown Military Collection, Brown University Library. Background, *Saratoga*, drawing, around 1783–1784, Francois Godefroy after a work by Fauvel, Library of Congress Prints and Photographs Division. **Page 4.** *Benedict Arnold*, painting, 1782, courtesy Clive Hammond of Gloucester, England. **Page 8.** Birthplace of Benedict Arnold, daguerreotype, 1851, E.Z. Webster, Library of Congress Prints and Photograph Division. **Page 10.** Cartouche from a map of Virginia done by Joshua Fry and Peter Jefferson, engraving, first done in 1754, Library of Congress Geography and Map Division. **Page 14.** Sign from Arnold's apothecary shop, eighteenth century, New Haven Colony Historical Society. **Page 15.** Leech jar, glazed pottery, eighteenth century, Rockefeller Library, Colonial Williamsburg Foundation. **Page 16.** Proof Sheet of 1d stamp duties for newspapers, 1765, Philatelic Collection, The British Library. **Page 19.** Benedict Arnold's house, New Haven, CT, photograph, late nineteenth century, Library of Congress Prints and Photograph Division. **Page 22.** *The Engagement at the North Bridge*, painting, 1775, Amos Doolittle, The New York Public Library, Astor, Lenox, and Tilden Foundations. **Page 24.** Map of Fort Carillon, 1777, Michel Capitaine du Chesnoy, Library of Congress Geography and Map Division. **Page 26.** *Working Against the Flood on Dead River*, engraving, 1903, drawn by Sydney Adamson and engraved by H. Davidson, Library of Congress Prints and Photograph Division. **Page 27.** *Capture of Fort Ticonderoga: Ethan Allen and Captain de La Place*, engraving, late nineteenth century, from a painting by Alonzo Chappel, North Wind Picture Archives. **Page 30.** A view of St. John's (spelled St. Johns in the text), engraving, 1789, Thomas Anburey, U.S. Naval Historical Center. **Page 35.** Map of Canada and the United States, 1778, Gilles Robert de Vaugondy, Library of Congress Geography and Map Division. **Page 37.** *Carrying the Bateaux at Skowhegan Falls*, engraving, 1903, drawn by Sydney Adamson, engraved by C. W. Chadwick, Library of Congress Prints and Photograph Division. **Page 40–41.** A view of Quebec City, watercolor and ink on paper, 1775, George Heriot, National Archives of Canada.

Page 42. *The Death of General Montgomery in the Attack on Quebec, December 31, 1775*, painting, 1786, John Trumbull, Francis G. Mayer/CORBIS. **Page 43.** See cover. **Page 45.** *Sir Guy Carleton*, engraving, 1783, Anne S. K. Brown Military Collection, Brown University Library, **Page 48–49.** *The Attack and Defeat of the American fleet Under Benedict Arnold*, engraving, around 1750, William Faden from a sketch taken by an officer on the spot, Library of Congress Geography and Map Division, **Page 49.** (*inset*) *Arnold's Engagement on Lake Champlain*, engraving, 1776. **Page 58.** *Governor William Tryon Arresting Regulators*, engraving, nineteenth century, North Carolina State Archive. **Page 60.** *John Burgoyne*, painting, 1766, Sir Joshua Reynolds, Frick Collection. **Page 62.** *Philip Schuyler*, painting, 1881, Jacob Lazarus, after a work by John Trumbull, Schuyler Mansion State Historic Site, New York State Office of Parks, Recreation and Historic Preservation. **Page 66–67.** See cover. **Page 71.** Arnold's oath of allegiance to the United States, 1778, National Archives and Records Administration, Old Military and Civil Records. **Page 72.** *Back of the State House, Philadelphia*, engraving, 1799, William Birch and Son, Independence National Historical Park. **Page 75.** *Margaret Shippen Arnold*, sketch, 1778, John André, Culver Pictures. **Page 80.** Coded letter from Benedict Arnold to John André, July 12, 1780, The Clements Library, University of Michigan Library. **Page 84.** Pass written by Arnold for Joshua Hett Smith and others, September 21, 1780, New York State Archives. **Page 85.** Orderly book from August 8–October 3, 1780, New-York Historical Society. **Page 87.** *Major John André*, sketch, 1780, self-portrait, Library of Congress Prints and Photographs Division. **Page 89.** *The Unfortunate Death of Major John André*, engraving, 1783, Goldar after a painting by Hamilton, The Clements Library, University of Michigan Library. **Page 96.** A proclamation by Brigadier-General Arnold to the officers and soldiers of the Continental army, broadside, 1780, printed by James Rivington, Library of Congress, Rare Books and Special Collections Division. **Page 98.** Plaque on Arnold family tomb at St. Mary's Battersea, England, Angelo Hornak Library.

Credits

Photo Credits

Project Editor
Daryl Heller

Series Design
Laura Murawski

Layout Design
Corinne L. Jacob

Photo Researcher
Jeffrey Wendt